D1544306

RON BOWMAN

LET US PRAY

A Minister's Prayer Book

Compiled by
PAUL D. LOWDER

The Upper Room
The World's Most Widely Used Devotional Guide
and
Other Devotional Literature
1908 Grand Avenue
Nashville 5, Tennessee

The Scripture quotations in this book are from the Revised Standard Version of the Bible, copyrighted 1946 and 1952 by the Division of Christian Education of the National Council of Churches, and are used by permission.

Library of Congress Catalog
Card Number: 63-13588

UR-181-15-0363
Printed in the United States of America

FOR MARTHA
WHO KNOWS HOW MUCH AND HOW LITTLE
THIS BOOK HAS HELPED

FOREWORD

Nearly fifteen years ago I began compiling a personal prayer book. It was not an original idea. I began it because I saw how much such a book meant in the life and ministry of a friend. Through the years the two of us have exchanged quotations which we have found helpful and recommended inspirational books to each other. To him I will always be indebted.

One of the most significant ways this book has helped me is that by rereading passages which meant something to me when I first read them, I have become familiar enough with them for God to use them over and over in speaking to me. It has been said that God usually speaks out of the background. This book has become a large part of the background for me. It has also been helpful in giving me an objective prayer list. I have not been able to pray adequately for others by means of blanket blessings; I need a prayer list.

I am grateful to those who have given permission to use quoted materials. When I have been unable to locate a source, I have designated it as unknown. Where no source is given, the material is my own. It is hoped that no copyright has been infringed upon. If it has, I offer my apology and will in the future give credit.

The title of the book is from the liturgical response:

> *Minister:* The Lord be with you.
> *People:* And with thy spirit.
> *Minister:* Let us pray.

Paul D. Lowder

Thanksgiving, 1962

Conover, North Carolina

CONTENTS

I. PREPARATION FOR PRAYER

How rare it is to find a soul quiet enough to hear God speak!
Fénelon (1)

"The only way to pray is to pray, and the way to pray well is to pray much. If one has no time for this, then one must at least pray regularly. But the less one prays the worse it goes."
Anonymous (2)

For God alone **my soul** waits in silence. . . .

Psalm 62:5.

Listener: I don't hear anything.
A Voice: No. You are in too great a hurry.
Listener: All right. I will listen. . . . I am listening. . . .
A Voice: No. You are talking. Keep quiet.
Listener: I am keeping quiet now. . . . Speak, Lord. . . .
A Voice: You are talking again. . . . Listen!
Listener: My soul, be thou silent unto God!

Source Unknown

There is nothing more important in any day than developing our friendship with God.

Robert Stackel (3)

If you are never alone with God, it is not because you are too busy; it is because you do not care for Him, do not like Him. And you had better face the facts.

Al-Ghazali (4)

3/9/75

You must at all costs have a quiet time. Give up work if need be. Your influence finally depends upon your own firsthand knowledge of the unseen world, and on your experience of prayer. Love and sympathy and tact and insight are born of prayer.

Forbes Robinson (5)

11/3/74

There is no hope but in prayer. Herein lies the Church's power against the world. Prayer is the main business of every day.

Andrew Bonar (6)

If we believe in prayer, we pray. If we do not believe in it, we do not pray.

Stanley Plunkett

The prayer of the morning will determine the day. Wasted time, which we are ashamed of, temptations that beset us, weakness and listlessness in our work, disorder and indiscipline in our thinking and our relations with other people very frequently have their cause in neglect of the morning prayer.

Dietrich Bonhoeffer (7)

For Christians the beginning of the day should not be burdened and oppressed with besetting concerns for the day's work. At the threshold of the new day stands the Lord who made it. All the darkness and distraction of the dreams of night retreat before the clear light of Jesus Christ and his wakening Word. All unrest, all impurity, all care and anxiety flee before him. Therefore, at the beginning of the day let all distraction and empty talk be silenced and let the first thought and the first word belong to him to whom our whole life belongs. "Awake thou that sleepest, and arise from the dead, and Christ shall give thee light." (Eph. 5:14.)

Dietrich Bonhoeffer (8)

The success of the work [of contemplation] much depends upon the frame of thy heart. . . . Get thy heart as clear from the world as thou canst. Wholly lay by the thoughts of thy business, troubles, enjoyments, and everything that may take up any room in thy soul. Get it as empty as thou possibly canst, that it may be the more capable of being filled with God. . . . There is no trifling with holy things.

Richard Baxter (9)

And now one word about prayer. It is a preparation for danger, it is the armor for battle. Go not, my Christian brother, into the dangerous world without it. You kneel down at night to pray, and drowsiness weighs down your eyelids. A hard day's work is a kind of excuse, and you shorten your prayer and resign yourself softly to repose. The morning breaks, and it may be you rise late, and so your early devotions are not done, or done with irregular haste. No watching unto prayer—wakefulness once more omitted. And now we ask, is that reparable? Brethren, we solemnly believe not. There has been that done which cannot be undone. You have given up your prayer, and you will suffer for it. Temptation is before you, and you are not fit to meet it. There is a guilty feeling on the soul, and you linger at a distance from Christ. It is no marvel if that day, in which you suffer drowsiness to interfere with prayer, be a day on which you betray Him by cowardice and soft shrinking from duty. Let it be a principle through life, moments of prayer intruded upon by sloth cannot be made up. We may get experience, but we cannot get back the rich freshness and the strength which were wrapped up in these moments.

Frederick W. Robertson (10)

After all, the very best thing one can do for one's neighbor as well as for God, is to keep spiritually alert, and *anything* which checks prayer is to be held in suspicion.

Evelyn Underhill (11)

It is dangerous to read a great deal *about* prayer, unless at the same time we are doing all we can to practice it.

Olive Wyon (12)

Prayer is not an easy way of getting what we want, but the only way of becoming what God wants us to be.

G. A. Studdert-Kennedy (13)

Prayer is my chief work, and it is by means of it that I carry on the rest.

Thomas Hooker (14)

Most of the casualties in the spiritual life are found at the place of a weakened prayer life.

E. Stanley Jones (15)

The reality of God for me depends upon my turning to Him, "waiting" upon Him, listening to Him.

Olive Wyon (16)

It is when preachers become popular (Mark 1:37) that they are in greatest danger of neglecting prayer; but it was when men most sought Christ that He most sought God. One may preach well without praying much if he but have the intellectual and oratorical gifts, but no one can preach effectually without praying much, for effectual preaching depends more on grace than on gifts.

Preparation for service is as important as the service itself.

W. Graham Scroggie (17)

While we deliberate, he reigns.
When we decide wisely, he reigns.
When we decide foolishly, he reigns.
When we serve him humbly, loyally, he reigns.
When we serve him self-assertively, he reigns.
When we rebel and seek to withhold our services, he reigns.

William Temple (18)

When the charge or care of anything rests upon you,
God ceases to be a God of peace.
Bear not a single care thyself;
One is too much for thee.
The work is Mine, and
Mine alone,
And thine is—
Trust in Me.

Source Unknown

A Prayer for the Spirit of Believing Prayer

Heavenly Father, who hast said that all things are possible to believing prayer, pour into our spirits such complete faith, that what we ask in Thy name shall be given to us.

Grant us such a passion for prayer that nothing will prevent us pleading the desires that Thou Thyself has put into our hearts.

We are sure that if we could pray this way, every other precious thing would come with it.

Give it to us! For our Saviour's sake.   Amen.

W. E. Sangster (19)

You can *do more* than pray *after* you have prayed, but you cannot do more than pray *until* you have prayed.

A Book of Prayers (20)

I. CONFESSION AND SELF-EXAMINATION

Do not be discouraged at your faults; bear with yourself in correcting them, as you would with your neighbor. Accustom yourself gradually to carry prayer into all your daily occupations. Speak, move, work in peace, as if you were in prayer.

Fénelon (21)

A Prayer of Confession

Dear Lord God, we cannot count the sins that we have done and are still doing. We have forgotten most of them and no longer feel our guilt. Whatever is in us and in every power besides grace is sin and condemned. Thus we must altogether despair of ourselves, our works, and our powers. We know not what else to do but to hope and pray for thy mercy. As far as grace and faith control us we are devout through Christ, but where these fail, we know and confess that nothing good is left in us. No matter how long we may live we shall never find it different. Though we had the holiness of all the saints, there would still be nothing good in what we think, speak, live, and do without thy divine grace and power. This is our joy and comfort which thou dost gladly grant poor sinners that all our sins are forgiven out of pure grace. Amen.

Martin Luther (22)

A Prayer of Confession

O almighty, eternal God of truth, Father of our Lord Jesus Christ, . . . We confess and are deeply sorry that we are sinful and have so often sinned against thee. We implore thee to forgive us all our sins, be gracious unto us, and justify us for thy beloved Son's sake, whom thou didst decree to be our Redeemer. With thy Holy Spirit, purify our hearts and guide our souls that we may truly know, adore, and be obedient unto thee, O God of truth, eternal Father, Son, and Holy Spirit. Keep thy one eternal church forever among us, and grant us good government, nourishment and happy homes. Mercifully guide and guard us and our poor children, that in this life we may worship in thy true church and in eternity be with thee and praise thee in wisdom, righteousness, and joy. Amen.

Philip Melanchthon (23)

A Prayer for Honest Self-Examination

Almighty God, since our minds have so many hidden recesses that nothing is more difficult than thoroughly to purge them from all pretense and lying, grant that we may honestly examine ourselves. Do thou also shine upon us with the light of thy Holy Spirit. May we truly acknowledge our hidden faults and put them far away from us, that thou mayest be our only God. May we offer thee pure and spotless worship, and conduct ourselves in the world with a pure conscience. May each of us be so occupied in our duties as to seek our brother's advantage as well as our own. At length make us partakers of that true glory which thou hast prepared for us in heaven, through Christ our Lord. Amen.

John Calvin (24)

An Act of Self-Examination

On the following pages are questions that will help you face your sins. This will require real honesty. It will not be painless. Before we can seek forgiveness we must become aware that we are sinful.

Each of us is an artist at disguising his sins. They are not pretty. But they are our sins!

Think of yourself as God's child, and recall how often you have not been willing to love Him.

Do not hurry. Do not worry if you cannot remember all your sins. Be honest with God and with yourself. This is what it takes to make a real confession.

Remember, you are seeking forgiveness, not more guilt. God is ready to forgive, but sometimes our pride keeps us from forgiving ourselves. "The Lord is near to the brokenhearted, and saves the crushed in spirit." (Psalm 34:18.)

1. Pride

"You shall have no other gods before me." (Exodus 20:3.)

Have I been more interested in self than in God?

Have I always tried to be on top?

Have I been unjustly proud of my church, its size, prestige or "influential" members? Have I been ashamed of my church, my ministry, or my members?

Have I considered myself better than others because I am a minister? Or because I have an education? Or because of some other advantage?

Have I talked too much about myself—about what *I* think, what *I* want?

Have I deliberately called attention to myself? Been sorry for myself? Thought that others had more luck? Refused to admit a mistake? Neglected to apologize? Thought I deserved what I have attained in life? Thought the world owed me a living because I am in religious work?

2. Idolatry

"You shall not make yourself a graven image, or any likeness of anything that is in heaven above, or that is on the earth beneath, or that is in the water under the earth; you shall not bow down to them or serve them." (Exodus 29:4-5a.)

Have I put other people before God?

Am I more concerned about what others think of me than am of what God thinks of me?

Is popularity and the desire for it coming between God and me?

Have I used religion, prayers, and my position to gain popularity?

Is my piety real?

Have I been concerned about clothes, cars, or things which are of secondary importance?

Have I been more aware of the people who hear my prayers than I have been aware of God?

3. PROFANITY

"You shall not take the name of the Lord your God in vain." (Exodus 20:7.)

Have I used profanity in order to impress the sophisticated? Or to prove that I am a "man"?

Do I give way to worry or needless concern instead of relying on God? Rather than press the panic button, do I think of God?

Have I had profane thoughts which were not expressed because I did not have enough courage?

4. IRREVERENCE

"Remember the sabbath day, to keep it holy." (Exodus 20:8.)

Have I purposely missed church when on vacation?

Have I learned to worship when visiting another church instead of being concerned about how the minister is leading the service, how the choir sings, and whether or not I could do a better job with the sermon?

Even though Sunday is not a day of leisure for me, is it in any sense spiritually refreshing? Do I limit myself on Sunday so that it will not be a day less holy to me than to others?

Have I, through the promotion of church programs, made it difficult for my people to rest on Sunday?

Am I irreverent in church? In the way I think of God's house?

5. Disobedience

"Honor your father and your mother." (Exodus 20:12.)

Am I grateful for what my parents have done for me? For their sacrifices, interest, and love?

Did I develop a willingness to be obedient in my relationship with them?

Have I been willing to contribute to the support of my parents?

Have I shown a lack of respect for the laws of the church? For the laws of the nation?

What about speeding on the highways?

What sins have I committed with regard to my wife and children?

Have I given as much care and attention to the religious life of my family as I have urged others to give?

Do I practice what I preach in my own home?

Have I seen that my children get religious instruction at home as well as at church?

How often have I tried to dominate the lives of others?

6. Hatred

"You shall not kill." (Deuteronomy 5:17.)

Have I killed anyone by my judgment of them? By my tongue? By desire?

Am I angry unjustly?

Do I hurt people with ridicule? With my refusal to accept them?

Do I repeat things about people without being sure they are true?

What about grudges and resentments? Am I willing to forgive?

How often has God had to forgive me? Has He ever failed to forgive?

Am I willing to help people who need help, even though they may have been foolish, or did not deserve help? To how many people am I indebted for help, though I do not deserve it?

What part have I played in tempting other people to sin?

7. IMPURITY

"Neither shall you commit adultery." (Deut. 5:18.)

Do I enjoy letting my imagination have free reign?
What about "smutty" stories? If they fascinate me, why?
Do I have a true Christian concept of sex?
How often do I neglect my family? My work?
Am I intemperate in my eating habits?
Does recreation re-create me? Is it escape or pure relaxation?
Do I get enough physical exercise? If not, am I neglecting to care for the temple?
Am I suspicious of other people's motives? What about my own?

8. THEFT

"Neither shall you steal." (Deut. 5:19.)

Have I stolen anything ever?
Have I been careless with other people's money?
Do I try to pay all my debts? To live within my income?
Do I believe that God has given me all I have? If so, am I grateful?
Has my tithing been faithful to my preaching of stewardship?
Have I stolen another person's good name, his rights or privileges?

9. DECEIT

"Neither shall you bear false witness against your neighbor." (Deut. 5:20.)

In my conversation have I exaggerated the facts? Have I been deceptive?

Do I add to all the stories I tell—as if they really happened that way?

How often have I let other people accept the responsibility for my mistakes?

Am I guilty of "passing the buck"?

Do I condemn sins of which I too am guilty? Do I condone those sins which I enjoy?

Have I told things about people that were true, but which I knew would hurt them?

Have I remained silent and thereby given a false impression?

Am I as interested in the welfare of others as I try to appear to be?

10. DISCONTENT

"Neither shall you covet. . . ." (Deut. 5:21.)

Of what am I jealous? Money? Prestige? Pastorates? Parsonages? Success? Popularity? Love? Independence?

Have I been jealous or resented attainments of brother ministers?

Do I enjoy seeing anyone in trouble?

Do I enjoy being discouraged? Do I indulge myself in thinking I am a martyr?

Can I accept loss or hard tasks gracefully?

Do I seek goodness for its own sake? Is righteousness as attractive as some other things?

Can I learn in my lifetime to be content with a few things?

How much will it take to make me happy? Or is there enough in what I already possess to do it?

In what special ways am I under judgment today?

If I believe that God is more concerned to reveal Himself to me than I am to Him; that He has an answer for every question; that He can mold me into His likeness; that He can meet my needs—why do I not give Him the opportunity to do so?

What about my sense of values?

> All that which pleases is but for a moment—
> All that which troubles is but for a moment—
> That only is important which is eternal.
> > —Over the three great doors into
> > Milan Cathedral

A Prayer for Forgiveness

Forgive me, dear Lord, for the sins that come to my remembrance when I turn to confession.

I have been slack in prayer and slow to witness.

I have shown resentment at criticism.

I have been irritable and impatient even over trifles. I have been self-indulgent and allowed words and feelings to get out of control.

I have quarreled and been slow to "make it up."

I have spread fear through my fearing and depression through my depression.

I have assessed the faults of others as worse than my own without due thought of my privileges and without knowledge of their hard way.

O Thou, before whom my heart is laid open and bare, forgive me and help me to do better.   Amen.

Let me now accept Thy forgiveness and forgive myself. Let me no longer cling to the picture of myself as unclean, when Thou Thyself, by forgiveness, hast made me clean. Help me not endlessly to condemn and deprecate and despise myself, but to understand myself and move on to spiritual maturity. Let me slip off my shoulders the old filthy rags and wear, as did the Prodigal, the new, shining raiment of a son. No atonement of mine, no expiation or propitiation is possible or necessary. Thou dost not ask me to atone but to accept *freedom* from the burden of guilt, so that the forgiven past becomes an asset in a dedicated future. Let me know now Thy forgiveness and help me from today to move forward. For Thy name's sake.   Amen.

Leslie Weatherhead (25)

Concerning the Spiritual Life:

1. Do you pray always?
2. Do you rejoice in God every moment?
3. Do you in everything give thanks—in loss, in pain, in sickness, in weariness, in disappointment?
4. Do you desire nothing?
5. Do you fear nothing?
6. Do you feel the love of God continually in your heart?
7. Have you a witness in whatever you speak or do, that it is pleasing to God?

John Wesley (26)

O Jesus, we thy ministers bow before thee to confess the common sins of our calling. Thou knowest all things; thou knowest that we love thee and that our hearts' desire is to serve thee in faithfulness; and yet, like Peter, we have so often failed thee in the hour of thy need. If ever we have loved our own leadership and power when we sought to lead our people to thee, we pray thee to forgive. If we have been engrossed in narrow duties and little questions, when the vast needs of humanity called aloud for prophetic vision and apostolic sympathy, we pray thee to forgive. If in our loyalty to the Church of the past we have distrusted thy living voice and have suffered thee to pass from our door unheard, we pray thee to forgive. If ever we have been more concerned for the strong and the rich than for the shepherdless throngs of the people for whom thy soul grieved, we pray thee to forgive.

O Master, amidst our failures we cast ourselves upon thee in humility and contrition. We need new light and a new message. We need the ancient spirit of prophecy and the leaping fire and joy of a new conviction, and thou alone canst give it. Inspire the ministry of thy Church with dauntless courage to face the vast needs of the future. Free us from all entanglements that have hushed our voice and bound our action. Grant us grace to look upon the veiled sins of the rich and the coarse vices of the poor through thine eyes. Give us thine inflexible sternness against sin, and thine inexhaustible compassion for the frailty and tragedy of those who do the sin. Make us faithful shepherds of thy flock, true seers of God, and true followers of Jesus. [Amen.]

Walter Rauschenbusch (27)

III. PRAYERS

May it be
Not my word aimed at my glory,
Nor Thy word aimed at my glory,
Nor my word aimed at Thy glory,
But Thy word, through me,
To Thy glory, through us all.
David Head (28)

A Morning Prayer

O God, give me strength to live another day. Let me not turn coward before its difficulties or prove recreant to its duties. Let me not lose faith in my fellowmen. Keep me sweet and sound of heart in spite of ingratitude, treachery, or meanness; preserve me from minding little stings or giving them; help me to keep my heart clean and to live so honestly and fearlessly that no outward failure can dishearten me or take the joy of conscious integrity; open wide the eyes of my soul that I may see good in all things. Grant me this day some new vision of thy truth; inspire me with the spirit of joy and gladness, and make me a cup of strength to suffering souls; in the name of the strong Deliverer, our only Lord and Savior, Jesus Christ.   Amen.

Phillips Brooks (29)

A Prayer for Inspiration

Almighty God, Father, Son, and Spirit, who art power, wisdom, and love, inspire in me these same three things: power to serve thee, wisdom to please thee, and love to do it; power that I may do, wisdom that I may know what to do, love that I may be moved to do all that is pleasing to thee.

Nun's Prayer (30)

A Prayer for Renewal of Confidence

O Lord, who art the guard and guide of all who put their trust in Thee, grant me Thy peace. Thou knowest the cares that torment my spirit; Thou seest the pathway of experiences which this day holds for me, and Thou art able to keep me in Thy strong hand through its fortune or misfortune.

Forgive the worries that sap my strength and cloud my thinking because I have so great difficulty trusting in Thee. Save me, Father, from anxious self-concern, and help me to give this day's activity to Thee, realizing that my efforts are a part of Thy great plan working out in history. All my mixed feelings of love and resentment, trust and doubt, belief and unbelief, I place in Thy hand, thankful that Thou dost love me as I am. Grant me the grace to use my problems to bless other people rather than hurt them.

Now let me walk forth with confidence because I claim Thee as my Father, and because, though unworthy, I accept myself as a son of Thy household, through Jesus Christ our Lord. Amen.

James T. Hall (31)

A Prayer for Courage

O Lord, quicken in me the spirit of courage. May I go forth to the duties and conditions of this day with a hopeful mind, confident that with thy help I can fashion something good out of whatever materials the day will provide. In Christ's name I pray. Amen.

* * *

There is no day in which one cannot exhibit courage and goodwill, and be a help instead of a hindrance to one's fellowmen.

Hugh Tigner (32)

A Prayer of Supplication

Grant to us, O Lord,
To know that which is worth knowing.
To love that which is worth loving,
To praise that which pleases thee most,
To value that which to thee seems precious,
To hate that which in thy sight is unclean. . . .
And above all
To be ever searching after the good pleasure of thy will. . . .
Through Jesus Christ our Lord. Amen.

Thomas à Kempis (33)

A Prayer of Thanksgiving

Thanks be to Thee, O Lord Jesus Christ, for all the benefits
which Thou hast given us; for all the pains and insults which Thou
hast borne for us. O most merciful Redeemer, friend and brother
may we know Thee more clearly, love Thee more dearly, and
follow Thee more nearly; for Thine own sake. Amen.

Richard of Chichester (34)

A Morning Prayer

O God, Who art the unsearchable abyss of peace, the ineffable
sea of love, the fountain of blessings, and the bestower of affec
tion, Who sendest peace to those that receive it; open to us this
day the sea of Thy love, and water us with the plenteous streams
from the riches of Thy grace. Make us children of quietness, and
heirs of peace. Enkindle in us the fire of Thy love; sow in us Thy
fear; strengthen our weakness by Thy power; bind us closely to
Thee and to each other in one firm bond of unity; for the sake
of Jesus Christ. Amen.

Syrian Clementine Liturgy (35)

The Prayer of One Who Is Critical

Our Father,

Forgive me for being critical,
For judging when I do not have all the facts,
For judging when I am not perfect,
For judging when the thing I judge is my problem too.

Remove from me the evil that makes me critical:

My own desires to be like the person I criticize,
The wrong in me which I condemn in others,
The feeling of inferiority that keeps me from accepting myself,
The blindness that keeps me from seeing myself as Thou dost see me,
The smallness that permits other people to irritate me.

Give me love enough

To love those who are not like me,
To love those who are not sure of themselves,
To love those who are misunderstood,
To love those whom I cannot understand,
To love those who cannot control their tongues.

Help me to grow

In patience—to wait while thou dost work,
In grace—to know that a thing does not have to be perfect before it can be used,
In forgiveness—to forgive myself so that I can forgive others.

May I so love that there will be no need for me to be critical.
Make me realize that criticism rarely accomplishes anything except to set up barriers.

In the name of Christ, who came not to condemn the world, but to save men.   Amen.

PRAYER FOR A SENSE OF HUMOR

We give Thee thanks, O Lord, that we are capable of having a sense of humor. Truly it is a gift of Thy grace.

Increase our ability to see the saving humor in every human situation. Give us the proper perspective to laugh at ourselves. Make real to us the joy that is rightfully ours as Christians.

Help us always to laugh with others and never at them.

Make us ever conscious of the Source of all happiness.

In the name of Christ, who could see humor in a camel's going through the eye of a needle. Amen.

He who sits in the heavens laughs. . . . (Psalm 2:4a.)

A PRAYER FOR RELIANCE UPON GOD'S WILL

O God, who art the guide and shepherd of all faithful souls, consecrate with thy presence the way our feet may go, and the humblest work will shine, and the roughest places be made plain. Lift us above selfishness and distrust into faith and hope and charity, by a simple and steadfast reliance upon thy holy will. In all things draws us to the mind of Christ, that we may be at one with thee. Amen.

Thomas Arnold (36)

A Prayer for Sunday Morning

Almighty God, today I must go forth to preach Thy Word. Have mercy on me and touch these unclean lips with holy fire. Thou hast called me to Thy service, knowing me for what I am. I am not worthy to speak for Thee. Thou hast forgiven me repeatedly; forgive again, Lord, so that I can go into that pulpit with a clean heart.

My preparation is not adequate. There is sin in the unfitness of my mind and soul. The neglect of the years condemns me. Had I listened more earnestly, thought more deeply, followed more faithfully, I should have heard Thy voice more clearly. So take the poor offering I bring this day and use it as only Thou canst.

Let me get out of the way, Lord, so that the people may see Thee, not me; hear Thee, not me.

Fill the house with heavenly power. Weave our adoration, praise, thanksgiving, prayer, and meditation into one great act of communion with Thee. Lift the burden from the heavy-laden; open the eyes of some blinded one; enter some heart; and strengthen Thy saints. Therefore, Father, speak now a gracious word through me to Thy people. In Thy pardoning grace behold Thy servant, and send me forth in Thy name, for Jesus' sake. Amen.

Leslie Davison (37)

A Prayer Before Preaching

Grant, our Father, that as I preach I may not be more interested in being in good taste than I am in being of use for Thee. Help me to consider nothing too simple to be of use to Thee, even though I should like something more erudite, sophisticated and scholarly.

Deliver me from preaching down to my people. Help me to speak to them as individuals, directly from Thy heart through mine.

Give me confidence without arrogance, and humility without fear.

May my preaching not be mere words; but let it be full of Thy love.

Help me always to hear Thy voice while I am preaching.

For the Master's sake. Amen.

****

Grant me, I beseech Thee, O merciful God, prudently to study, rightly to understand, and perfectly to fulfill that which is pleasing to Thee, to the praise and glory of Thy name.

Thou, O Christ, art the King of glory; Thou art the everlasting Son of the Father. Amen.

Thomas Aquinas (38)

A SACRISTY PRAYER

O Lord God, dear Father in heaven, I am indeed unworthy of the office and ministry in which I am to make known Thy glory and to nurture and to serve this congregation.

But since Thou hast appointed me to be a pastor and teacher, and the people are in need of the teachings and the instructions, O be Thou my helper and let Thy holy angels attend me.

Then if Thou art pleased to accomplish anything through me to Thy glory and not to mine or to the praise of man, grant me out of Thy pure grace and mercy a right understanding of Thy Word, and that I may also diligently perform it.

O Lord Jesus Christ, Son of the living God, Thou Shepherd and Bishop of our souls, send Thy Holy Spirit that He may work with me, yea, that He may work in me to will and to do through Thy divine strength according to Thy good pleasure. Amen.

Martin Luther (39)

A Prayer "For Hearing God's Word"

Almighty God, as nothing is better for us or more necessary for our chief happiness than to depend on thy Word (for that is a sure pledge of thy goodwill toward us), grant that, as thou hast favored us with so singular a benefit, we may be attentive to hear thee and submit ourselves to thee in true fear, meekness, and humility. May we be prepared in the spirit of meekness to receive whatever proceeds from thee, and may thy Word not only be precious to us, but also sweet and delightful, until we shall enjoy the perfection of that life which thine only-begotten Son has procured for us by his blood. Amen.

John Calvin (40)

A Prayer "For Greater Spirituality"

Behold, Lord, an empty vessel that needs to be filled. My Lord, fill it. I am weak in faith; strengthen thou me. I am cold in love; warm me and make me fervent that my love may go out to my neighbor. I do not have a strong and firm faith; at times I doubt and am unable to trust thee altogether. O Lord, help me. Strengthen my faith and trust in thee. In thee I have sealed the treasures of all I have. I am poor; thou art rich and didst come to be merciful to the poor. I am a sinner; thou art upright. With me there is an abundance of sin; in thee is the fullness of righteousness. Therefore, I will remain with thee of whom I can receive but to whom I may not give. Amen.

Martin Luther (41)

A Prayer for Fellow Prisoners
(Christmas, 1943)
Morning Prayers

O God,
Early in the morning do I cry unto thee,
Help me to pray.
And to think only of thee.
I cannot pray alone.

In me there is darkness,
But with thee there is light.
I am lonely, but thou leavest me not.
I am feeble in heart, but thou leavest me not.
I am restless, but with thee there is peace.
In me there is bitterness, but with thee there is patience;
Thy ways are past understanding, but
Thou knowest the way for me.

O heavenly Father,
I praise and thank thee
For the peace of the night.
I praise and thank thee for this new day.
I praise and thank thee for all thy goodness
and faithfulness throughout my life.
Thou hast granted me many blessings:
Now let me accept tribulation
from thy hand.
Thou wilt not lay on me more
than I can bear.
Thou makest all things work together for good
for thy children.

Lord Jesus Christ
Thou wast poor
and in misery, a captive and forsaken as I am.
Thou knowest all man's distress;
Thou abidest with me
when all others have deserted me;
Thou dost not forget me, but seekest me.
Thou willest that I should know thee and
turn to thee.
Lord, I hear thy call and follow thee;
Do thou help me.

O Holy Spirit,
Grant me the faith that will protect me from
despair; deliver me from the lusts of the flesh.
Pour into my heart such love for thee and for men,
that all hatred and bitterness may be blotted out.
Grant me the hope that will deliver me from fear
and timidity.

O Holy, merciful God,
my Creator and Redeemer,
my Judge and my Savior,
Thou knowest me and all that I do.
Thou hatest and dost punish evil without respect to persons
in this world and the next.
Thou forgivest the sins of them that
heartily pray for forgiveness;
Thou lovest goodness and rewardest it on this earth
with a clear conscience, and in the world to come
with the crown of righteousness.

Chiefly do I remember all loved ones,
my fellow prisoners, and all who
in this house perform their hard service.
Lord have mercy.
Restore me to liberty,
and enable me so to live now,
that I may answer before thee and before the world.
Lord, whatever this day may bring,
Thy name be praised.
Amen.

Dietrich Bonhoeffer (42)

THE PRAYER OF AN OLD SLAVE

Father,
I ain't what I want to be,
I ain't what I ought to be,
I ain't what I'm going to be,
But thank you, Father,
I ain't what I used to be.

When you are too tired to think, when you are too tired to meditate, when you are too tired to pray, when you are too tired to go to sleep, use the great prayer, "the master prayer." There is only one word to it. Just say, "Jesus." Pray it over and over. That will do more to cleanse your inner mind than any other word in the universe. I say that honestly and through experimental knowledge.

Harold A. Tassell, M.D. (43)

IV. INTERCESSION: PRAYER LISTS

I know as a minister that I have failed
my people most, not in my preaching or
pastoral work, but in my prayer.
W. E. Sangster (44)

Intercessory prayer might be defined as
loving our neighbor on our knees.
Charles Brent (44a)

The chief obstacles to intercession are moral. We live for what we can get; our dominant desires are selfish. . . . Even when we do succeed in praying for our friends, our country, or the Kingdom, we are often giving lip-service to conventionality. . . . *Intercession is the result of generous devotion, not of logical analysis.* When such devotion comes into the life of any man who vitally believes in God, like a rising stream in a dry river bed it lifts the obstacles at whose removal he had tugged in vain, and floats them off. The unselfish prayer of dominant desire clears its own channel. We put our *lives* into other people and into great causes; and our prayers follow after, voicing our love. . . .

Harry Emerson Fosdick (45)

Dear Lord, grant that no person may fail in his hour of temptation or trial because I have not prayed for him.   Amen.

On this page list the members of your immediate family.

MARY JANE

TIM

ANDY

MARK

PETER

STEVIE

JOSEPH

A Prayer for a Married Couple

O God, our heavenly Father, protect and bless us. Deepen and strengthen our love for each other day by day. Grant that by Thy mercy neither of us ever say one unkind word to the other. Forgive and correct our faults, and make us instantly to forgive one another should one of us unconsciously hurt the other. Make us and keep us sound and well in body, alert in mind, tender in heart, devout in spirit. O Lord, grant us each *to rise to the other's best*. Then we pray Thee add to our common life such virtues as only Thou canst give. And so, O Father, consecrate our life and our love completely *to Thy worship*, and to the service of all about us, especially those whom Thou hast appointed us to serve, that we may always stand before Thee in happiness and peace; through Christ our Lord. Amen.

Bishop Charles Lewis Slattery (46)

INTERCESSION FOR MINISTERS

On this page write the names of your bishop, synod president, or others with whom you work. Also, list ministers for whom you wish to pray regularly.

BISHOP REUBEN MILLER ✱ RALPH
DR. KENNY FORBES + T.
DR. ROBERT FRIBLEY ALTON
DR. EVAN BERGWALL RICHARD
DR. L. G. SAPP THISTLE
REV. HERSCHEL DYER JIM MORIN
+ MARGE
REV. LOREN TODD DR. WESLEY
BRANSFORD
REV. HARRY HUFFMAN & WIFE
REV. WAYNE BAXTER & TOM CAPIN
REV. RUSSELL DAWSON RALPH
REV. ERNEST SHOEMAKER JANKA
RAY BACHMAN
REV. AUGGIE LUNDQUIST DARRELL
TAGGART
BISHOP RICHARD C. RAINES YUNG CHEN
BILL MOODY STAN TOBIAS CHARLIE
RILEY CASE HIK

45

A Prayer for Ministers

I lift up my heart, O God, for all ministers of the Gospel, that those who feel successful may lay hold again on the humility of Christ and realize their dependence on Him and that those who feel failures may lay hold on His patience and realize that His claim is only on their faithfulness and obedience. Grant that both may care for Christ's opinion more than any opinion of man.

So for all ministers may this day be one of quiet and happy service in His dear name, with neither laziness nor fussy, over anxious bustling, but fulfilling the demands of their ministry in the order of importance which the values of the kingdom suggest leaving that which is honestly impossible today until the morrow without worry or fear of men.

Grant that all ministers of Thy holy Gospel may live in such close communion with Thee that radiant living may win men to seek Thee, and passionate pleading may win men to follow Thee So may the ministries of all denominations enable Thee to extend Thy glorious kingdom in the hearts of men, and find their unity with one another in serving that one great cause, the dwelling together in Thine all-embracing love. For Jesus Christ' sake. Amen.

Leslie Weatherhead (47)

On this page list those persons who are a problem for you—those you find it difficult to love, those you dislike, those who may dislike you.

DON EYER

Be specially kind and patient with those who irritate you! And make of this effort an offering to God. Instead of wasting energy in being disgusted with yourself, accept your own failures and just say to God, "Well, in spite of all I am, say, or fancy, this is what I am really like—so please help my weakness." This, not self-disgust, is the real and fruitful humility.

Evelyn Underhill (48)

List below special needs as they arise in the lives of those you know. List your own special needs. List those persons who need healing, physically, mentally, or spiritually. List those persons for whom you think no one is praying.

Don Egee

Alan Boxell
Greg Wilson
"Red" Anderson
Bill Clampitt
Marilyn Douglas
Lee Kinzer
Dawn Kinzer
Kay Woods
Bruce Kenline
Ron Verlee

Best of all, however, God is a loving person. The reason he began the world and created everything within it is because of his love. He loves everybody everywhere all the time.

John B. Coburn (49)

48

On this page list those whom you want to be won for Christ.

Sangster's Seven Rules for Personal Evangelism

1. Get to live at the center yourself.
2. Do not set out to make people good—love them.
3. Miss no opportunity of doing people a service, and if you cannot do them a service, ask them to do one for you.
4. When you speak about our Lord, speak naturally.
5. Speak about Jesus and not so much about yourself.
6. When speaking of Jesus, speak positively.
7. Persist in your contacts until you win your man.

W. E. Sangster (50)

On this page list some of the names of members of your church. It is almost impossible to pray for each member each day, but most churches are small enough that you can pray for each member at least once a week. A complete list of your church members might be kept close at hand and reviewed before you pray. Do not just have a roll call each day, but think of the needs of your church members—their weaknesses, their strengths, and their hopes—and present these to God.

Give me grace, Lord, to stop thinking of my people as church members who ought to act like Christians, and help me to think of them as sinners who want to be saints. Amen.

V. GOALS

Brethren, I do not consider that I have made it my own; but one thing I do, forgetting what lies behind and straining forward to what lies ahead, I press on toward the goal for the prize of the upward call of God in Christ Jesus. (Philippians 3:13-14.)

For my part, and I have been long at it, I desire no other gift of prayer than that which ends in making me a better and better woman. By its fruits your prayer will be known to yourselves and others.

Teresa of Avila (51)

A MORNING RESOLVE

I will try this day to live a simple, sincere and serene life, repelling promptly every thought of discontent, anxiety, discouragement, impurity, self-seeking; cultivating cheerfulness, magnanimity, charity, and the habit of holy silence; exercising economy in expenditure, generosity in giving, carefulness in conversation, diligence in appointed service, fidelity to every trust and a childlike faith in God. . . . In particular I will try to be faithful in those habits of prayer, work, study, physical exercise, eating and sleep, which I believe the Holy Spirit has shown me to be right.

And as I cannot in my own strength do this, nor even with a hope of success attempt it, I look to thee, O Lord my Father, in Jesus Christ my Saviour, and ask for the gift of the Holy Spirit.

Anonymous (52)

Whenever you ask humbly, without deciding in advance that some answers are unacceptable, and are patiently confident that God's timing is perfect, then you can be sure of His guidance through life. He may use friends or enemies. He may slam some doors until you are strong enough to hear the answers, or experienced sufficiently to understand them, or humble enough to receive them. It was so with Jesus, and it will be so with you.

Archie Matson (53)

The Distinctive Characteristic of a Minister

The distinctive characteristic of a minister *per se* is that he has a sure word about God. He can go to the pain-wracked and nourish the faith in them that love is at the heart of all things. He can go to the dying and take the terror (though not the awe) from death. He can go to the bereaved and put comfort right in the core of their heart. He doesn't just "repeat the words." He is sure—and he can communicate something, at least, of his assurance to others. This is his special task. Some laymen have it too, but the minister ought to have it above all. If he's not eloquent, or a "hearty," or a "genius" with youth, or a "superb" administrator, forgive him. He has a sure word about God. He's a minister! And if he hasn't a sure word about God, will it matter very much if he's all the other things? He fails at the very point he's appointed to meet. He's not a minister.

Where does that assurance come from? From God Himself, of course. How does it come? Not in our college lectures—though much that is precious comes that way. Not at our ordination—solemn and wonderful though that hour is meant to be. It comes from much private fellowship with God in prayer.

W. E. Sangster (54)

Do I have that sure word?

If we believe what Jesus said, it means . . . that whoever loves you, *God loves you more.* Whoever believes in you, hopes and dreams of your future, loves to have your confidence and friendship, *God cares more.* Whoever can help, guide, strengthen, enable, enrich you, *God can more.*

Rita Snowden (55)

It has been coming ever clearer to me that what we *are* is so infinitely more important than what we do: that what we do at its best is only a reflex of what we are: that the big business of life is not to crowd more and more into our days (my own lifelong error) but to be in our small way an incarnation of our Lord. No day is a failure in which Jesus has really indwelt us: no day is a success (however effective in a worldly sense) in which His reflection in us has been badly blurred.

The aim, then, is so to order one's thinking: so steadily to hold the mirror of one's life up to the Lord, that all my life becomes a reflection of His. Then one preaches without words: love informs all one's doings, and the slightest contact with another is capable of imparting the Lord.

W. E. Sangster (56)

The supreme prayer of my heart is not to be rich, famous, powerful or "too good," but to be radiant. I desire to radiate health, calm courage, cheerfulness, and goodwill. I wish to live without hate, whim, jealousy, envy, or fear. I wish to be simple, honest, frank, natural, clean in mind and clean in body, unaffected, ready to say, "I do not know," if so it be, to meet all men on an absolute equality, to face any obstacle and meet every difficulty unabashed and unafraid. I wish others to live their lives, too, up to their fullest and best. To that end I pray that I may never meddle, interfere, dictate, give advice that is not wanted, or assist when my services are not needed. If I can help people, I will do it by giving them a chance to help themselves; and if I can uplift or inspire, let it be by example, rather than by injunction and dictation.

That is to say, I desire to be radiant—to radiate life.

Source Unknown (57)

You must not expect to make adjustment to the pastorate in a brief time. It takes time to become acquainted with people and really learn to love and appreciate them. You also have to learn many things the hard way, and often by trial and error, but the training is profitable, and the compensations are greater than any you have yet experienced.

Howard P. Powell

In many cases, walking with Jesus may not make much difference in what the preacher says, but it will make a great deal of difference in the influence of what he says. Whether the pastor is in his study, visiting in his parish, or in his pulpit, he must be free from the frustration of bondage. He must not be living under the cloud of conscience that keeps condemning him for not praying more or visiting more or studying more. He must have release from the tiring monotony of the spiritless service which makes him indolent and lazy. He must be free from the delusion that he is overworked or in a particularly difficult field. He is where God has put him, with sufficient strength to do what God wants him to do. He needs the wisdom to do all this, just this and no more. All of this comes naturally as he walks with Jesus.

Wesley W. Nelson (58)

We ought not to try and be more religious than God himself.
Dietrich Bonhoeffer (59)

When a man really gives up trying to make something out of himself—a saint, or a converted sinner, or a churchman (a so-called clerical somebody), a righteous or unrighteous man . . . when in the fullness of tasks, questions, success or ill-hap, experience and perplexities, a man throws himself into the arms of God . . . then he wakes with Christ in Gethsemane. That is faith, that is *metanoia* and it is thus that he becomes a man and Christian. How can a man wax arrogant if in a this-sided life he shares the suffering of God?

Dietrich Bonhoeffer (60)

COMMENDING OTHERS TO GOD

I find it perfectly easy to commit my own life to God and to ask Him to show me what to do with it, but I find to my dismay that when I try to commend to God the life of a young person who is as dear to me as _____ is, I find myself trying to keep one hand on the reins too—as though God were not quite capable of managing without me. Foolish, is it not? But we can pray for him, and you know I will do that constantly.

Winifred Bateman

Let our lives be spent simply in working for God. It is almost impossible for most of us to live without distractions, telegrams, telephones, letters, and so on, and when we live in a perfect rush, narrow practices cannot be carried out. . . . Working for God gives such a reality to life. . . . No matter what you are doing or how you are doing it, in itself it is not the value of a grain of sand. . . . It is only *grace* that counts. On your knees in prayer, or eating your dinner, no matter. If God doesn't wish you to do it, being in the Chapel isn't a bit better thing to do than eating your breakfast. . . . The one thing that concerns us is, Am I doing this for God? . . . I do it because it is God's will and so He is pleased, and it simplifies life wonderfully.

Father Daniel Considine (61)

If I do not have time enough to do it well, God does not want me to do it.

Howard P. Powell

RIGHT KNOWLEDGE

I wish a greater KNOWLEDGE than to attain
The Knowledge of myself; a greater *Gain*
Than to augment myself; a greater *Treasure*
Than to enjoy myself; how slight and vain
Is all self-knowledge, pleasure, treasure, gain;
Unless my better KNOWLEDGE could retrieve
My CHRIST; unless my better Gain to thrive
In CHRIST; unless my better Pleasure pitch
On CHRIST; or else my KNOWLEDGE will proclaim
To my own heart, how ignorant I am:
Or else my Gain, so ill improved, will shame
My trade, and show how much declined I am:
Or else my Treasure will but blot my name
With Bankrupt, and divulge how poor I am:
Or else my Pleasures, that so much inflame
My Thoughts, will blab how full of sores I am:
Lord, keep me from my SELF, 'tis best for me
Never to own my SELF, if not in Thee.

Francis Quarles (62)

Two things above all hinder our spiritual growth. On the one hand, our fretful concern about the state of our soul's health and on the other, our self-seeking impulses which in spite of all our prayer and meditation on God's Word, in spite of all our attempts at self-improvement, ever lurk within us, driving us to take ourselves more seriously than God, to consider our honor as more important than the honor of God, so that our pride refuses to bend beneath the yoke of the humility of Christ. As long as we are thus worldly and self-willed Christ cannot take form and shape within us.

Emil Brunner (63)

We are all tempted to justify our boorishness and inconsiderateness of others on the plea that we are "busy with important things"—or that we are "practical"—or that we are (blessed word) "sincere"! Let us be honest. *There is never any excuse for bad manners.* To be great is to be gracious; to be good is to be kind; to be holy is to walk in the joy of the Lord and to impart it to others.

Bestow on me, O Lord, a genial spirit and unwearied forbearance; a mild, loving, patient heart; kindly looks, pleasant, cordial speech and manners in the intercourse of daily life; that I may give offense to none, but as much as in me lies live in charity with all men.

Johann Arndt (64)

You Will Not Be Sorry

For hearing before judging,
For thinking before speaking,
For bridling an angry tongue,
For stopping the ears to a talebearer,
For disbelieving most of the ill reports,
For being kind to the distressed,
For being patient toward everybody,
For doing good to all men,
For being courteous to all.

Source Unknown

When we are in one stage of experience we should never look down upon people who are at another stage, and all of us must never doubt for a moment that whatever experience we have, if we receive it rightly, is wholly and entirely for our blessing, our education, our growth in holiness. It is how we receive it that matters. Life brought to our Lord the lilies of the field, and He said, "Consider the lilies how they grow! Our heavenly Father has clothed them with glory greater than the glory of Solomon." Life brought to Him the thorns, and He twisted them into the crown of a king. He received the loveliness of the lilies and the cruelty of the thorns, and if anything the thorns gave Him more glory than the lilies. "As a rose among the thorns," says a verse of Scripture. It is how we receive what God gives us, and not really what He gives us, that is to be our concern. What he gives us is His will: whatever He gives us, if we receive it with faith and love, will promote our growth in holiness. The advice one would give to anyone going through a wilderness or along a lonely road when the evening was falling, would be "Plod on!" and that is the best advice for these stages of the spiritual journey we are talking about now. "Plod on!"

H. E. Hardy (65)
(Father Andrew)

61

But here lies the secret. Christ gave it. He said words to this effect, "When you are tempted to criticize or resent, turn your attention to yourself and leave your brother alone." Recognize the beam of resentment and criticism in yourself, let the Holy Spirit deal with that, then you will be fitted to deal with your brother's mote. For either you will cease to notice it and it will be swallowed up in your renewed vision of all there is of Christ in him, or you will recognize that your Lord, who tenderly removes your faults in His own way, is also his Lord, who will do the same for him without your interference; or if in a rare case you are led to speak, it will be more a word of confession of your resentment than rebuke for his failure.

In other words, the first great secret of maintaining unity is—the moment I am inclined to criticize or resent a brother, I must recognize my spirit of criticism as the sin which concerns me and not my brother's behavior: and I must keep on letting God deal with it till a spirit of appreciative love replaces it, by which I honour my brother instead of judging him, and rejoice in all of the image of Christ to be seen in him.

Norman Grubb (66)

DISAGREEMENTS

Someone has offered ten practical rules for dealing with those with whom we differ:

1. I will always seek to discover the best and strongest points in my brother's position.
2. I will give him credit for sincerity.
3. I will not listen to gossip and secondhand information.
4. I will avoid classifying him, and assuming that he has all the characteristics of the class to which he is supposed to belong.
5. I will emphasize our agreements.
6. When others criticize, I will try to bring out favorable points.
7. When there is misunderstanding, either I of him or he of me, I will go to him direct, if possible.
8. I will try to remember that God's truth is too big for any one mind.
9. I will never ridicule another's faith.
10. I will pray for those with whom I differ.

Lord, help me always to put myself in another's place, and to try to find a way to reconciliation through understanding.

Light Upon the Road (67)

The little act of obedience, love, self-restraint, meekness, patience, devotion, offered to you actually, is all you can do now and if you neglect that to fret about something else at a distance you lose your real opportunity of serving God. A moment's silence when some irritating words are said by another, may seem a very small thing; yet at that moment it is your one duty, your one way of serving and pleasing God, and if you break it, you have lost your opportunity.

H. L. Sidney Lear (68)

Through every event, however untoward, there is always a way through to God.

Dietrich Bonhoeffer (69)

The bigger we are in our own eyes, the smaller God is; where as, when we are little in our own sight, God is sufficient for the greatest emergency.

Liu Shand Ch'en (70)

"Wherever Jesus Christ is, there anything can happen." *And He is with me!*

E. Stanley Jones (71)

Everybody will not agree with me, neither will I agree with everyone. Therefore, by the grace of God and with His love in my heart, I purpose to disagree agreeably, cheerfully, kindly, and lovingly.

Howard P. Powell

Usually, when God speaks, He speaks through a human voice that is kind. Nothing stops the sound of His voice so quickly as criticizing, carping, unkindness.

Andrew W. Blackwood, Jr.

Every temptation to evil temper which can assail us today will be an opportunity to decide the question whether we shall gain the calmness and the rest of Christ, or whether we shall be tossed by the restlessness and agitation of the world.

F. W. Robertson (72)

To be wronged is nothing unless you continue to remember it.

Confucius

65

If thou wilt withdraw thyself from superfluous words, and from unprofitable runnings-about, and from hearing of rumors and of vain tales, thou shalt find time convenient to be occupied in holy meditations.

Thomas à Kempis (73)

Thou art a preacher of the Word; mind thy business.

Old Puritan (74)

Lord, teach me to seek Thee, and show Thyself to me as I seek: for I cannot seek Thee unless Thou teach me, nor find Thee unless Thou show Thyself.

Anselm of Canterbury (75)

Blessed is the man who loveth Thee, and his friend in Thee, and his enemy for Thee.

Augustine of Hippo (76)

But open your eyes and the world is full of God.

Jacob Boehme

It is impossible for the preacher to keep his spirit in harmony with the divine nature of his high calling without much prayer.

E. M. Bounds (77)

The leading defect in Christian ministers is want of a devotional habit.

Richard Cecil (78)

If you have Christ in your heart, you are a missionary. If you do not have Christ in your heart, you are a field for missions.

Filomena Natividad (79)

3/23/75

Talking to men for God is a great thing, but talking to God for men is greater still. He will never talk well and with real success to men for God who has not learned well how to talk to God for men.

E. M. Bounds (80)

Any hour of any day may be made perfect by merely choosing.
It is perfect if one looks toward God that entire hour, waiting for
his leadership all through the hour and trying hard to do every
tiny thing exactly as God wishes it done, as perfectly as possible.
No emotions are necessary. Just the doing of God's will perfectly
makes the hour a perfect one. And the results of that one perfect
hour, I believe, will echo down through eternity.

Frank Laubach (81)

I am sure God has something to teach us in every situation in
which we are put, and through every person we meet; and once
we grasp that, we cease to be restless, and settle down to learn
where we are.

Evelyn Underhill (82)

God tells me where the need is greatest the amount of love
needed is greatest too; and just loving people without always
being critical of them does more for them than all the preaching
at them.

Mary Webster (83)

There is no moment at which God does not present himself
under the guise of some suffering, some consolation, or some duty.

J. P. de Caussade (84)

68

Don't be afraid of "surface interests." Christ will be with you in those sorts of surface interests if they are wholeheartedly undertaken for His sake, and not for your own soul's sake.

These are the sort of things of a disciplinary kind which I think you ought to do. You have lost the knack of drawing strength from God: and vain strivings after communion of the *solitude a deux* sort will do nothing for you at this point. Seek contact with Him now in the goodness and splendour which is in other people, in *all* people, for those who have the art to find it.

But censoriousness and exclusiveness are absolute bars to making discoveries of that kind and you will not be happy till they are eliminated from your character. . . .

Evelyn Underhill (85)

I can well believe that the greater part of what you achieve will be unseen by you now and will bear fruit later. It needs much faith and love to accept that and carry on all the same in *a spirit of loving confidence*. But that is the way, I fancy, that God's hardest jobs are done.

Evelyn Underhill (86)

Goals for Attending a Ministers' Conference

1. *Above all,* keep daily quiet time. This may be the most diffi cult place on earth to keep it.
2. Say nothing to degrade or dishonor another minister, even i it is true! It will not help anyone, nor improve another' opinion of you by contrast.

"I shall never close the doors of opportunity to any membe of my conference by speaking a word unkindly about a brothe minister or his family, but on the other hand I shall endeavo to open doors of opportunity by hunting for the good an magnifying it whenever I have occasion to speak of m brethren."

Bishop W. W. Peele

3. Do not allow what others say to get you upset about your ap pointment—you will get one!
4. Allow nothing to make you hurry. "Hurry is the death o prayer"—and of a lot of other things: kindness, manners charity, patience, etc.
5. Realize the brotherhood. If it is not real for others, it still car be for you.

Anonymous (87)

"The best thing we can do for those we love is to help them tc escape from us" (Von Hügel). Very hard, but true—and more-over the best way to keep all the pure and noble enduring part of love. I want you to accept all the events and deprivations of your life because God is in them; and all the pains and struggles connected with your great power of loving and longing to give yourself, because these are the very disciplines and purifications that power of loving needs if it is to be useful to Him.

Evelyn Underhill (88)

As a minister, it is human to question whether or not I am in the place God wants me to be. Especially is this true if I belong to a denomination which appoints pastors instead of "calling" them. The best answer I have ever found is that given by Dr. Albert Edward Day. Once he was asked if he believed that God's will always prevailed in the appointment system. He said, "Of course not, but I am sure that wherever you are sent you can learn there the thing God wants you to learn at this time in your life."

My poise and peace of mind are more important than any sermon I can ever preach. Therefore I refuse to let my sermon preparation or lack of it upset me to the extent that it makes me difficult to live with or to love and be loved.

From now on when I have "kept my peace" and have not wasted my time, but done the best I can, I will not be overly-concerned about my sermons. When I have misused time or not had a balanced experience which has left me tired or with too little recreation, I will accept forgiveness and depend on God for support and strength.

I will remember that I am not preaching to make an impression or to prove that I can preach, but that I am speaking for God! And although I do not always feel like doing it, I shall leave the results to Him, with whom they are anyway.

Unless He gives the message, the poise and strength with which to deliver it, the sermon will be of little consequence.

Two Questions for Testing

1. How am I doing with Jesus Christ?
2. Is this for God, or is this for self?
   a. If it is for God, we try to do it.
   b. If it is for self, we do not do it.
   c. If we do not know, we wait.

Gertrude Behanna (89)

Watch Out for the Pedestal!

One of the best things you as a minister can do for your people is to get down off the pedestal. As long as your people can keep you there, they will believe in two standards of behavior—one for you and one for them. But when you get off the pedestal, they have to face the fact that you are facing the same daily problems they face; that you also are having to "slug it out" day by day. They cannot easily avoid the truth that if you can do it where they live, then they too must try!

Get off the pedestal!

Gertrude Behanna (90)

I do not think you have ever made the Cross the center of our life really. I do not quite know what you have made the center, but it looks as though it cannot be that. And you have got to, you know. Nothing else will do. And if you do not accept it deliberately, why then it will be forced on you in some subtle and ingenious way, as it is at the present moment. And by struggling and tiring yourself out, you make it worse and add physical and mental fatigue to your spiritual troubles. Accept what you are having, quite simply and obediently. Take it as it comes. Do not "will" or "want" this or that; however virtuous and edifying your wishes may be. All such willings presuppose that you know better than the Spirit of God. And do not get into a despairing condition. These experiences are a perfectly normal part of the spiritual life: which is not designed on the lines of a "Pleasant Sunday Afternoon."

Evelyn Underhill (91)

He is no fool who gives what he cannot keep to gain what he cannot lose.

Elisabeth Elliot (92)

The following things need attention in my life. With God's help, I will do something about them.

I believe that God is leading me to do the following. With His help, I will do these things:

O Lord, help me to be willing and determined to be led by Thee. Amen.

VI. THANKSGIVING AND PRAISE

Christ in the heart of every man who thinks of me,
Christ in the mouth of every man who speaks to me,
Christ in every eye that sees me,
Christ in every ear that hears me.
                              St. Patrick of Ireland (93)

It is good to give thanks to the Lord,
to sing praises to thy name, O Most High;
to declare thy steadfast love in the morning,
and thy faithfulness by night,
to the music of the lute and the harp,
to the melody of the lyre,
For thou, O Lord, hast made me glad by thy work;
at the works of thy hands I sing for joy. . . .

Psalm 93:1-4.

O God, we praise thee, we give thanks unto thee for thy bountiful providence, for all the blessings and all the hopes of life. Above all we praise and adore thee for thine unspeakable gift in thine only Son our Lord and Savior, Jesus Christ. Let the memory of thy goodness, we beseech thee, fill our hearts with joy and thankfulness to thee; through Jesus Christ our Lord. Amen.

Therefore with angels and archangels, and with all the company of heaven, we laud and magnify Thy glorious Name, evermore praising Thee, and saying: Holy, holy, holy, Lord God of Hosts, heaven and earth are full of Thy glory. Glory be to Thee, O Lord, most high! Amen.

If we do not give thanks daily for the Christian fellowship in which we have been placed, even where there is no great experience, no discoverable riches, but much weakness, small faith, and difficulty; if on the contrary, we only keep complaining to God that everything is so paltry and petty, so far from what we expected, then we hinder God from letting our fellowship grow according to the measure and riches which are there for us all in Jesus Christ.

This applies in a special way to the complaints often heard from pastors and zealous members about their congregations. A pastor should not complain about his congregation, certainly never to other people, but also not to God. A congregation has not been entrusted to him in order that he should become its accuser before God and men. When a person becomes alienated from a Christian community in which he has been placed and begins to raise complaints about it, he had better examine himself first to see whether the trouble is not due to his wish dream that should be shattered by God; and if this be the case, let him thank God for leading him into this predicament. But if not, let him nevertheless guard against ever becoming an accuser of the congregation before God. Let him rather accuse himself for his unbelief. Let him pray God for an understanding of his own failure and his particular sin, and pray that he may not wrong his brethren. Let him do what he is committed to do, and thank God.

Dietrich Bonhoeffer (94)

But be filled with the Spirit, addressing one another in psalms and hymns and spiritual songs, singing and making melody to the Lord with all your heart, always and for everything giving thanks in the name of our Lord Jesus Christ to God the Father.

Ephesians 5:18b-20

List here those things, persons, experiences for which you are thankful, especially those through which God has made Himself more real to you.

OR THE FATHERHOOD OF GOD

O Thou great Father of us all, we rejoice that at last we know thee. All our soul within us is glad because we need no longer cringe before thee as slaves of holy fear, seeking to appease thine anger by sacrifice and self-inflicted pain, but may come like little children, trustful and happy, to the God of love. Thou art the only true father, and all the tender beauty of our human loves is the reflected radiance of thy loving kindness, like the moonlight from the sunlight, and testifies to the eternal passion that kindled it.

Grant us growth of spiritual vision, that with the passing years we may enter into the fulness of this our faith. Since thou art our Father, may we not hide our sins from thee, but overcome them by the stern comfort of thy presence. By this knowledge uphold us in our sorrows, and make us patient even amid the unsolved mysteries of the years. Reveal to us the larger goodness and love that speak through the unbending laws of thy world. Through this faith make us the willing equals of all thy other children.

As thou art ever pouring out thy life in sacrificial father-love, may we accept the eternal law of the cross and give ourselves to thee and to all men. We praise thee for Jesus Christ, whose life has revealed to us this faith and law, and we rejoice that he has become the first-born among many brethren. Grant that in us, too, the faith in thy fatherhood may shine through all our life with such persuasive beauty that some who still creep in the dusk of fear may stand erect as free sons of God, and that others who now through unbelief are living as orphans in an empty world may stretch out their hands to the great Father of their spirits and find thee near.

Walter Rauschenbusch (95)

Thy Love*

O God, I praise Thee for Thy love, that which Thou art and without which Thou couldst not be the God of man. Thy love controls and shapes Thy power so that Thy almighty hand never slips in its creative task, but makes all things well. Thy love melts Thy disciplines into the gold of spiritual treasure, and distills the soft rain of compassion from the clouds of trouble. Nothing can escape the transfiguring touch of Thy love. Under its reign the darkness becomes as the light and the unseemly face of evil flees away in shame and defeat. O God, I praise Thee for Thy love which bathes me, even me. Amen. (96)

Discipline

Praise God for His disciplines. It is good for me that I have been in trouble. Thy chastisement has brought me to myself, so that I can see the depth and enormity of my sin, and the height and grandeur of Thy forgiving compassion. Thy terrors have suffered with a troubled mind, but out of the austerities of Thy love have come visions of hope and encouragement. My sin is ever before me, but of Thy mercy hast Thou forgiven sin. I praise Thee, my God, that Thou dost show me how bad I am in order that I may see how good I may be. I praise Thee that Thou dost not chastise to destroy but to build up and save to the uttermost. Behold, happy is the man whom God correcteth. (97)

---

* These meditations (numbers 96-104) are from Bishop Charles Henry Brent's *My Little Book of Praise*. They appeared in the *Historical Magazine of the Protestant Episcopal Church* in June, 1958, and are used by permission.

The Joy of Life

All is not dark. There is always sunshine somewhere, for which praise God—the sunshine that brightens other lives when mine is wrapped in gloom. Glory to Thee, my God, for the gladness of little children, for the joy of mothers, for the bliss of lovers. The radiance of their hearts is from Thy touch, because in the joy of Thy creation Thou rejoicest. And I praise Thee, my God, that in my unhappiest days there are breaks in the clouds through which I see the blue beyond and the glorious sun of Thy compassionate love. Even a moment of light gives me new hope and new courage to bear the stripes inflicted by my own sins. Praise the Lord. (98)

Opportunities

I praise Thee, my Lord God, for my opportunities of yesterday and the opportunities of today. In them I see Thee beckoning with Thy right hand and bidding me enter a door opened into heaven. Thou dost dwell in the midst of opportunity to possess it for us that we may enter in and make it our own. Yesterday, I but half seized my inheritance, failing to take it by force, that Kingdom which only yields to force. Today, my God, I would praise Thee for the opportunity that gives me bruised feet and bleeding hands as I move to embrace it. Let my praise declare its measures by my fortitude and patience and loyalty even to the end. Praise the Lord. (99)

THE CHURCH

Lord, Thy bride is my mother. I praise Thee that of her is my spiritual birth. When I was a puling babe, she gathered me in her arms and presented me to Thee for safekeeping. All her precious gifts, prayer and song and sacrament, have been mine. At her bosom have I been fed with nourishment to make me strong for conflict and sure for victory. Her arms, restless with love, reach through the great world of men to gather into Thy family and hers those who are far off and nigh. Wounded by her children, she never fails to tend and heal the wounded. Broken by angry voices within her family circle, she ever counsels peace. Shamed by rents in her beautiful seamless robe, she covers her confusion by renewed service. Lord, I praise Thee for Thy Church that is and for Thy Church that is to be. (100)

HOPE

Now, Lord, what is my hope? Truly, my hope is even in Thee. Yea, my hope is even Thee. Thou art all promise. In the darkest night Thy star is there to cheer and guide. Hope is power to see a tomorrow containing in it more of good than the today. It is the vision of the end and some purpose of love which makes the lover and the loyal super-victors through Thee who loved us and gave Thyself for us. I thank Thee for the hope of pardon, which over and again has saved me from despair in hours of bitter self-reproach and led me where the streams of living, cleansing water flow. I praise Thee for the hope of a better world bound together by unity of spirit in the bond of peace. I praise Thee for the hope that we shall one day clearly see Thy face and share in the fullness of Thy life. (101)

A Happy Day

Lord, this day has been one glad song through all its fleeting hours. Thou hast been my near companion, pouring Thy friendship into my soul. Though at the moment I related not always Thy gift to Thee, now in the evening shadows in each I find Thee the giver. Thou, the arbiter of the world which Thou didst make, art the lover of such a least child of Thine as I. Lord, make many the hours in which I am conscious of Thy nearness and ministering love. Especially reveal Thyself to me in the joys and pleasures of life, that I may use them for and with Thee. Summer fades, the summer of life, and winter comes, the winter of death. If I have learned to know Thee in the day, I cannot fail, when night falls, to know also that the night is Thine. (102)

Deserved Suffering

"What glory is it, if, when ye sin, and are buffeted for it, ye shall take it patiently?" (I Peter 2:20.) It is of Thy mercy, my righteous and loving Judge, that Thou dost not abate Thy chastisement for my sins. Thy lash is the lash of love, therefore it is my simple duty to praise Thee even when the pain of punishment is sore. Sin is disease: punishment is remedy. I praise Thee for the fitness of all the disciplines which have followed on my trespasses. Lord, help me not to fear them but to embrace them and to kiss the cross of Thy loving justice. I would pray Thee for one favor —that the penalties that are wholly mine should not be visited on others to their hurt. If they too must share innocently what I bear justly, let mystic power transfigure their pain until there comes to them clear shining after rain. (103)

"This is acceptable if for conscience toward God a man endure griefs, suffering wonderfully. If when ye do well, and suffer for it, ye shall take it patiently, this is acceptable to God." (I Peter 2:19-20.) I do thank Thee, my God, for opportunity to bear pain for others. Father, forgive them: they know not what they do. I praise Thee for giving me this opening to exercise forgiving love. Grant that I may shield those who have been unfair to me and to take with quiet thankfulness and open arms the humiliation that may come for the sake of Him who His own self bare our sins in His body upon the tree. That suffering, O Christ of the Agony, is in itself conquest and victory. Whatever place in my life it may have, I rejoice for it and praise Thee for it. Keep me steadfast that I may not fall into the trap of self-justification.

(104)

WE BELONG TO THEE

Father in Heaven! Draw our hearts to Thee, that our heart may be where our treasure must be, that our thoughts may aspire to Thy kingdom where our citizenship is so that our departure when Thou shalt call us may not be a painful separation from this world but a blissful reunion with Thee. Still we do not know the time or the season; perhaps it is still far from us. But when at times our strength is taken from us, when lassitude overcomes us like a kind of fog in which our vision is plunged as into a dark night, when our desire, our impatience, and our anger are stirred up, when our hearts tremble in anxiety awaiting what is to come, then, O Lord our God, teach us and strengthen this conviction in our hearts, that also in this life we belong to Thee. Amen.

Soren Kierkegaard (105)

WE SEEK THEE AT THIS HOUR

Father in Heaven! Our thought is turned toward Thee: again it seeks Thee at this hour, not with the unsteady step of a lost traveler but with the sure flight of a bird homeward bound. Grant then that our confidence in Thee be not a fugitive thought, a momentary leap, a mistaken appeasement of the heart and flesh. Grant that our aspirations toward Thy Kingdom, our hopes for Thy glory, be not unproductive birth pangs or waterless clouds, but that from the fullness of our heart they will rise toward Thee, and that being heard they will quench our thirst like the refreshing dew and satisfy us forever like Thy heavenly manna. Amen.

Soren Kierkegaard (106)

A Confession of God's Glory

When I seriously consider, great God, my dependence upon Thy providence, and that the favors and mercies I have received are infinitely more in number than the acknowledgments I have made, I am justly ashamed of my ingratitude, and afraid lest my unthankfulness should provoke Thee to hinder the current of Thy blessings from descending upon me.

Forgive me, O merciful Father, my past negligences, and give me grace for the time to come to observe and to value Thy kindnesses, as becomes one who has received so much more than he deserves. . . .

It is the desire of my soul, and shall be my great endeavor, that this life, which Thou hast preserved, should be dedicated to Thy immediate service, to which, by my repeated vows, I have bound myself: that we, whom Thou hast preserved, may serve Thee all our days.

Preserve in my soul, dear God, such a constant and clear sense of my obligations to Thee, that upon the receipt of every favor, I may immediately turn my eyes to Him from whom cometh my salvation. That Thy manifold blessings may fix such lasting impressions upon my soul, that I may always praise Thee faithfully here on earth, until it shall please Thee, of Thy unbounded mercy, to call me nearer the place of Thy heavenly habitation, to praise my Lord and Deliverer to all eternity. Amen.

Bishop Thomas Wilson (107)

A Prayer of Thanksgiving

O Lord God Almighty, Father of thy Christ thy blessed Son, who art ready to hear them that with uprightness call upon thee, and who knowest the petitions of them that are silent, we yield thee thanks for that thou hast vouchsafed unto us to partake of thy holy mysteries, which thou hast given unto us, for the fulfilment of good resolutions, for the preservation of piety, and for the remission of transgressions; because the name of thy Christ hath been called over us, and we have been enrolled in thy family. Thou who hast separated us from fellowship with the ungodly, unite us with those who have been sanctified to thee, establish us in the truth by the descent of the Holy Ghost; that which we do not know do thou reveal; that which is wanting do thou fill up; in that which is known to us do thou strengthen us; preserve thy priests blameless in thy service; maintain kings in peace, and rulers in righteousness; preserve the atmosphere in a good temperature, the fruits of the earth in fertility, the world in thy all-powerful providence. Soften the nations that delight in war, turn back that which has gone astray; hallow thy people; guard the virgins; keep married people faithful; strengthen the continent; bring infants to riper years; confirm the newly baptized; instruct the catechumens; cause them to become worthy of initiation, and lead us all into the kingdom of heaven, through Christ Jesus our Lord, with whom to thee and to the Holy Ghost be glory, honor, and worship for ever.   Amen.

The Clementine Liturgy

STILLNESS AFTER PRAYER

Be still, and know that I am God. (Psalm 46:10.)

But you are not still. You say your prayers, but before God has time to answer you are up from your knees and off.

It is the ten minutes after prayer that matters, the ten minutes during which, if we will wait, the answer will come from heaven. "I will hearken what the Lord will say concerning me." We never do that; we tell Him all our wants, but as one has said lately, we chatter like children to their parents, and never stay to hear what the parents say.

We are children, too, and we are not still. We do not hear what the answer is. We do not wait to hear what it is.

It may be that for years God has been trying to say something to us, but we have never given Him time to speak to us.

The Bishop of London (108)

VENI, CREATOR SPIRITUS

Come, Holy Ghost, our souls inspire,
And lighten with celestial fire.
Thou the anointing Spirit art,
Who dost thy sevenfold gifts impart.
Thy blessed unction from above
Is comfort, life, and fire of love.
Enable with perpetual light
The dullness of our blinded sight.
Anoint and cheer our soiled face
With the abundance of thy grace.
Keep far our foes; give peace at home;
Where thou art guide, no ill can come.
Teach us to know the Father, Son,
And thee, of both, to be but One;
That through the ages all along
This may be our endless song:
Praise to thy eternal merit,
Father, Son, and Holy Spirit.   Amen.

SOURCES

(The numbers correspond to the numbers given in parentheses
at the end of each selection.)

1. Quoted in D. A. McIntyre, *The Hidden Life of Prayer* (London: The Family Worship Union, Marshall, Morgan, and Scott, Ltd.), p. 40.
2. Quoted by Olive Wyon, *The School of Prayer* (London: SCM Press, 1943), p. 11. Source not given.
3. Source unknown.
4. Quoted by Gerald Kennedy in *A Reader's Notebook* (New York: Harper and Brothers, 1953), p. 105.
5. Quoted in *The Pattern of Prayer* by W. E. Sangster and Leslie Davison (London: The Epworth Press, 1962), p. 119. Used by permission.
6. Source unknown.
7. *Life Together* (New York: Harper and Row, 1954), p. 71. Used by permission.
8. *Ibid.*, p. 43.
9. *The Saints' Everlasting Rest.* Chapter XIII.
10. *Sermons* (New York: Harper and Row, n.d.), pp. 431-432. Used by permission.
11. *Letters.* Edited by Charles Williams. (New York: Longmans, Green and Co., 1943), p. 304. Used by courtesy of David McKay Co., Inc.
12. *Op. cit.*, p. 126.
13. Source unknown.
14. Quoted by Harry Emerson Fosdick in *The Meaning of Prayer* (New York: Association Press, 1956), p. 65. Used by permission.
15. *Christian Maturity* (New York: The Abingdon Press, 1957), p. 302. Used by permission.
16. *Op. cit.*, p. 15.
17. *Daily Notes.* The Scripture Union. Toronto, Canada. July 21, 1955.
18. Source unknown.
19. Quoted by Paul Sangster in the biography of his father, W. E.

Sangster, which is entitled *Doctor Sangster* (London: The Epworth Press, 1962), p. 232. Used by permission.

20. *A Book of Prayers,* published by the Auxiliaries of the United Lutheran Church. Used by permission of the United Lutheran Church Women. P. 4.

21. Quoted by Harry E. Fosdick, *op. cit.,* p. 73.

22. *Prayers of the Reformers,* edited by Clyde Manschreck. Copyright 1958 by The Muhlenberg Press, Philadelphia, Pa. Used by permission. P. 30.

23. *Ibid.,* p. 147.

24. *Ibid.,* p. 53.

25. *A Private House of Prayer,* pp. 175-176. Copyright 1958, by The Abingdon Press. Used by permission of Leslie D. Weatherhead.

26. Source unknown.

27. *Prayers of the Social Awakening,* pp. 81-82. The Pilgrim Press, Boston, 1910. Used by permission.

28. *Stammerer's Tongue,* p. 13. (London: The Epworth Press, 1960.)

29. Source unknown.

30. Quoted by Roland Bainton in *The Church of Our Fathers* (New York: Charles Scribner's Sons, 1950), p. 100.

31. Chaplain, Sibley Memorial Hospital, Washington, D. C.

32. Source unknown.

33. Source unknown.

34. *Prayers of the Middle Ages,* p. 70. Edited by J. Manning Potts, The Upper Room, Nashville, Tennessee, 1954. Used by permission.

35. *Prayers of the Early Church,* p. 16. Edited by J. Manning Potts, The Upper Room, Nashville, Tennessee, 1953. Used by permission.

36. Source unknown.

37. Sangster and Davison, *op. cit.,* p. 128.

38. *Prayers of the Middle Ages,* p. 70.

39. Ascribed to Martin Luther, but not found in his *Works.*

40. Manschreck, *op. cit.,* p. 79.

41. *Loc. cit.*

42. *Prisoner for God* (New York: The Macmillan Co., 1948), pp. 67-69. Used by permission.

43. *The Evangel Magazine* (now *Faith at Work*), June, 1950.

44. *Teach Me to Pray*, p. 11. Copyright 1959, by The Upper Room, Nashville, Tennessee.
44a. *Good Treasure*, Day 16. Forward Movement Publications, Cincinnati 2, Ohio. Used by permission.
45. *Op. cit.*, pp. 192-193.
46. Forward Movement Publications, Cincinnati 2, Ohio. Used by permission.
47. *Op. cit.*, pp. 99-100.
48. *Op. cit.*, p. 252.
49. *Prayer and Personal Religion* (Philadelphia: The Westminster Press, 1957), p. 13.
50. Paul Sangster, *op. cit.*, p. 162.
51. Quoted in *The School of Prayer*, p. 44.
52. *Forward Day by Day* (Forward Movement Publications, Cincinnati 2, Ohio). Used by permission.
53. *A Month with the Master* (New York: Harper and Row, 1958), p. 31. Used by permission of the author.
54. Sangster and Davison, *op. cit.*, p. 122.
55. *Through Open Windows* (London: The Epworth Press, 1956), p. 100.
56. Paul Sangster, *op. cit.*, p. 253.
57. Source unknown. Found near Tours, France, in 1918, and probably written by an A. E. F. doughboy in World War I.
58. *Show Me the Way*, p. 47. The Christian Literature Crusade. Used by permission.
59. *Prisoner for God*, p. 86. Used by permission.
60. *The Cost of Discipleship* (New York: The Macmillan Company, 1948), p. 19. Used by permission.
61. Wyon, *op. cit.*, p. 44.
62. Quoted by Adalbert R. Kretzmann in *The Pastor at Prayer*, p.v. Published by the Augsburg Publishing House, Minneapolis, Minnesota, 1957.
63. *The Great Invitation*, p. 148. Tr. Harold Knight. Published by the Westminster Press, Philadelphia, Pennsylvania. 1955. Used by permission.
64. *Forward Day by Day*, September 24, 1957. Used by permission.
65. *In the Silence*, pp. 11-12. Published by A. R. Mowbray and Co., Ltd., 1947. Used by permission.

66. *Touching the Invisible*. Christian Literature Crusade, p. 44. Used by permission.
67. *Light Upon the Road*, p. 16. Forward Movement Publications, Inc. Cincinnati 2, Ohio. Used by permission.
68. *Joy and Strength*, p. 200. Edited by Mary W. Tileston (New York: Grosset and Dunlap, 1929).
69. *Prisoner for God*, p. 84.
70. Source unknown.
71. *Christian Maturity*, p. 347.
72. Source unknown.
73. *The Imitation of Christ*.
74. *A Minister's Prayer Book*, edited by John W. Doberstein. P. 192. Published by the Muhlenberg Press, Philadelphia, n.d. Used by permission.
75. Quoted by Evelyn Underhill, *op. cit.*, p. 332.
76. Source unknown.
77. *The Preacher and Prayer*, p. 23. Published by the Zondervan Publishing House, Grand Rapids, Michigan, 1946.
78. *Ibid.*, p. 77.
79. Quoted in Sangster and Davison, *op. cit.*, p. 78.
80. *Op. cit.*, p. 26.
81. *Letters by a Modern Mystic* (Westwood, N. J.: Fleming H. Revell Co., 1938), p. 19.
82. *Op. cit.*, p. 173.
83. Quoted by E. Stanley Jones in *Growing Spiritually* (New York: The Abingdon Press, 1953), p. 280.
84. Source unknown.
85. *Op. cit.*, p. 98.
86. *Ibid.*, pp. 219-220.
87. Found in the New Mountain View Lodge, Lake Junaluska, North Carolina, June 9, 1962.
88. *Op. cit.*, p. 230.
89. In a talk to ministers, January, 1962. Used by permission.
90. *Ibid.*
91. *Op. cit.*, p. 120.

92. *Shadow of the Almighty* (New York: Harper and Row, 1958), p. 15.

93. From St. Patrick's breastplate. Found in several sources, but the complete text can be found in *The Catholic Encyclopaedia*, Vol. XI, p. 556.

94. *Life Together*, pp. 29-30.

95. *Prayers of the Social Awakening*, pp. 45-46. Used by permission of The Pilgrim Press, Boston, Massachusetts. Copyright 1910.

96-104. *The Historical Magazine of the Protestant Episcopal Church*, Vol. XXVII, No. 2, June, 1958. Used by permission.

105. *The Prayers of Kierkegaard*, p. 30. Edited by Perry LeFevre. The University of Chicago Press, 1956. Used by permission.

106. *Ibid.*, p. 55.

107. *Sacra Privata*, p. 95.

108. *A Book of Prayers*, p. 5.